50p.

D0783687

a passion for

Handbags

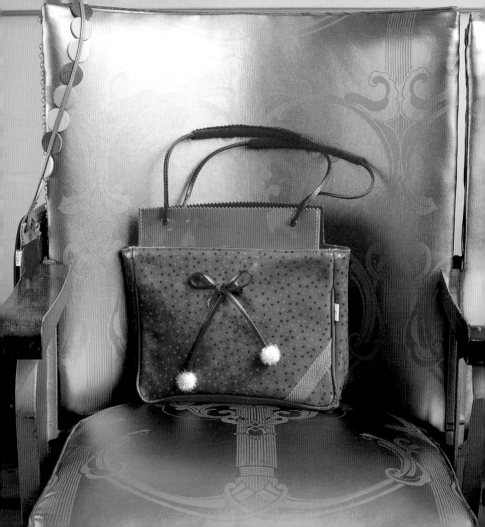

a *passion* for

Handbags

Emma Bowd

RYLAND
PETERS
& SMALL
LONDON   NEW YORK

Designer Luis Peral-Aranda
Editor Miriam Hyslop
Location Research Manager Kate Brunt
Production Tamsin Curwood
Art Director Gabriella Le Grazie
Publishing Director Alison Starling

First published in the United Kingdom in 2002
by Ryland Peters & Small
20–21 Jockey's Fields, London WC1R 4BW
www.rylandpeters.com

10 9 8 7 6 5

Text © Emma Bowd 2002
Design and photographs © Ryland Peters
& Small 2002

Printed and bound in China

ISBN 1 84172 354 1

A CIP record for this book is available from
the British Library.

contents

Handbags are hypnotic, spell-binding little creatures that entice a significant number of women into their world. The sheer volume of them in our wardrobes is testament to the fact that we seem to be totally incapable of resisting the seduction of their charms.

first handbags

*H*andbags are grown-up versions of our childhood fascination with all brightly coloured objects that glisten and gleam, open and close, and sparkle and sway. It is a fact much maligned by those politically correct new mums, that darling little girls will always choose the pretty pink, fluffy, sequinned Barbie handbag over the ergonomically designed and environmentally friendly toddler backpack. And handbag designers know that we never grow out of this! They constantly lure us with an endless array of shiny clasps, slinky straps, bold buckles, exotic textures, prettily patterned fabrics, fringing, beading, stitching, and magical secret chambers.

one size fits all

Any diehard handbag lover knows only too well the pleasure of purchasing a gorgeous, gleaming handbag. The mere fact that the two of you are joined in this happy union gives you instant, calorie-free joy. Moreover, you don't need to worry about trying it on with fingers and toes crossed in the vain hope that it will fit you. Handbags never let you down! Whether your style is tote or clutch, vintage or cutting edge, high street or Hermès, your stunning new handbag will be admired and envied long before anyone notices the size of your thighs or the bad hair day that you may be experiencing. What better fashion accessory could a woman want?

big is beautiful

The appeal of handbags rests in the very fact that they are beautiful, so they make us feel beautiful. Their outward appearance allows us to maintain a certain semblance of fashion credibility too, irrespective of whether inside nestles a silk Fendi make-up bag and gold embossed Smythson diary, or half-eaten toddler biscuits and baby wipes. No one need ever be the wiser! And the bigger our handbags are, the more we can hide inside them. We all have friends who carry around what could easily amount to their entire life's belongings in their trusty sacks, ready for whatever eventuality may come their way. Or, if you are a Parisian,

it may be your perfectly coiffed pet poodle that takes pride of position in your handbag! Many of us have a big, loyal work bag too. This is the one constant companion that is never far from our sides, with all the lumps, bumps and scratches to prove its

bags of style

devotion. These bags meet our needs so perfectly, in both the fashion and function stakes, that we find it hard to live without them. They always have good solid straps that are undeniably comfortable to wear for long periods of time and durable enough to withstand being jostled and jammed in peak-hour train rides. A secure zip to deter prying hands is almost always a prerequisite. The fact that it effortlessly matches numerous pairs of shoes (both winter and summer) adds further to its longevity as your number one bag. Usually, no matter how many times we try to substitute another handbag for our current long-standing work bag, we always end up returning to the same old faithful friend. At times, we will need to employ the operation of a 'dual handbag' system, whereby we take an additional, smaller and more fashionable handbag to work with us for important lunch-time meetings and evening dinner dates.

the favourite bag

Most of us can admit to having one special handbag amidst the masses in our wardrobe which has the esteemed status of being our favourite. This type of bag has many guises, changing shape and colour from season to season, month to month or even week to week depending on our latest whim. Your 'current' favourite is usually a very beautiful handbag that instantly transforms last season's outfits with its up-to-the-minute styling and colours. Like the pink and tangerine felt bowling bag from a cutting-edge new designer which is the perfect size to carry the exact amount of items you need to survive your day. Or the brilliant

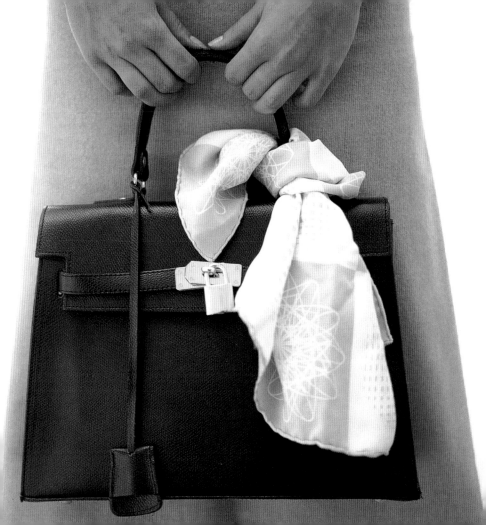

fire-engine red mock-croc shoulder bag with pencil-thin straps that makes those long mid winter days so much more bearable. It could also be the huge tote bag that goes everywhere with you, whose versatility enables seamless transitions between office, gym, lunch dates and shopping trips. And it is always exciting when you delve into the abyss of its inner reaches only to discover a favourite lipstick that you haven't seen in months! Or, your favourite handbag may very well be the bag that has never actually seen active duty on your arm, spending its days making your dressing table look really beautiful instead. Like the exquisitely beaded evening bag, which caught your eye in the sale bin of an expensive store, that you could not walk past because it was your favourite colour and when you looked at the label it was actually named after you. For the truly besotted handbag lover, the all-time favourite handbag is no more than an elusive dream. A handbag so desired that waiting lists of up to six months are the norm. Some handbags, like the coveted Kelly bag, even require one to be invited onto the list, surely the goal of every obsessed bag lover!

the evening bag

Evening bags personify the sheer indulgence, beauty and glamour of the special occasion you have gone to all the trouble of attending. Their sole purpose is to be the jewel in the crown of your outfit. Ensure you relish every moment of such a rare and exciting opportunity to delve into this exotic, fabulously feathered world. And the more silk, satin and sequins used the better. Whether you opt for a crystal-encrusted clutch, a slinky metallic mesh pouch, or something dainty with bejewelled handles or gleaming clasps, you will be sure to sparkle all night long. But most of all the size of your evening bag must not be much bigger than a tube of lip-

stick. You will, of course, be compelled
to squeeze your extra bits and bobs
into your partner's suit jacket pocket!

the vintage bag

There is one very big advantage to painstakingly looking after your handbags and storing them away when they're out of date. If you keep them long enough and resurrect them at just the right time, they enter the hallowed arena of the 'vintage handbag'. Vintage bags ooze class, confidence and style. Don't cave in to the pressures of feng shui by throwing out all of those piles of handbags in the bottom of your wardrobe. Instead, pack them up and forget about them for 20 years. Your daughters will love you for it when today's fashion goes through the inevitable 'retro' phase, and they will have an enviable collection of delightful vintage handbags to choose from.

What more beautiful family heirloom could a girl ask for? A passion for vintage handbags can also provide us with very special experiences, like the magical thrill of rummaging through an obscure thrift shop and stumbling upon the most exquisite handbag you

timeless treasures

have ever seen. And of course there is the fascinating speculation about what sort of life your discovery may have had before your paths crossed. The owner, the parties, the dresses, the shoes – all a truly unique mystery and mystique that lives on forever.

the designer bag

The dedicated handbag lover will usually succumb to at least one of the three popular types of designer handbag. First, there is the obvious logo-emblazoned handbag that announces to the world, in all its bold glory, your immediate membership of a very special club. Logos range from discreet metal clasps to boldly tattooed symbols that cover the bag. Importantly, these handbags are also the only fashion items in our wardrobes which make it acceptable, even desirable, to arrive at a party carrying an identical accessory to that of someone else. Secondly, there is the handbag produced by the talented, upmarket designer who has carved out a certain

'look' or 'style', without the need for visible logos. This type of bag certainly sorts out the true handbag devotees from the logo junkies, and is always greatly admired and appreciated for its subtle beauty. The third type of designer handbag is the 'one-off' handmade

crème de la crème

variety – the crème de la crème of hand-bags, which are unique in their design and exquisite in their craftsmanship. They are living displays of the artisan's skills in the use of materials, and leave the mass-produced bags lagging a long way behind in any competition.

the holiday bag

The most exciting part about packing for your long-anticipated summer holiday is rummaging through the deepest depths of your wardrobe to choose which one of the seven 'holiday' bags (all bought on previous trips) you will take with you. Whether it's your Biarritz market canvas carry-all, or your woven raffia Spanish beach basket, these bags are characteristically cavernous in size. And they all remind you of sunny, carefree times abroad in exotic locations. If you find the prospect of lugging a huge rustic bag through city airport check-ins too daunting, then there are always the upmarket designers to save the day with their

stunning range of summer holiday bags. These bags are the centrepiece of the chic beach holiday wardrobe. From these collections you can create a vast array of seamless ensembles - perfectly matching shoes, bikinis, sarongs and hats - which will make

handbag therapy

you blend in effortlessly to that St Tropez boulevard. The ultimate holiday destination for the handbag devotee is a weekend of shameless retail therapy in Florence. Allow plenty of space in your case and you can return home with a divine assortment of elegant bags!

the perfect match

Every handbag fan knows only too well that bags are an integral part of our female social fabric. The vast array of colours, shapes, textures and styles at our fingertips means that no day need go by without the best handbag to complement our current mood, age and budget – from solid, square power bags, to slinky, mesh evening bags, timeless couture treasures and savvy, streetwise totes. At last, handbag designers have worked out that when we go shopping to buy a coffee mug we often come home with a yellow daisy appliquéd 'bag of the season' instead! Whatever the life event, you can be sure that a suitably noteworthy handbag is at the

centre of your memories. Like dancing around them in discos with a gaggle of girlfriends, blowing your first 'real' pay packet on a 'must-have' designer bag or attending your first glittering black-tie ball. When occasion calls, rarely is an eyebrow raised at the indulgent

decadence

purchase of a gorgeous black suede rhinestone-encrusted handbag with matching shoes and belt. And what better way to make a statement of coordinated wedding chic than by commissioning a bespoke hat and hand-bag from your favourite designer?

suppliers & stockists

Accessorize
www.accessorize.co.uk
stores nationwide

Anya Hindmarsh
15–17 Pont Street
London SW1X 9EH
t. 020 7838 9177
www.beabag.com

Bill Amberg
10 Chepstow Road
London W2 5BD
t. 020 7727 3560
www.billamberg.com

Chanel
26 Old Bond Street
London W1S 4QD
t. 020 7493 5040
www.chanel.com

Christian Dior
31 Sloane Street
London SW1X 9NR
t. 020 7235 1357
www.dior.com

Fenwick
New Bond Street
London W1A 3BS
t. 020 7629 9161
www.fenwick.co.uk

Furla
31 New Bond Street
London W1S 1DF
t. 020 7629 9827
www.furla.com

Gucci
t. 020 7471 4199 for stores
www.gucci.com

Harrods Ltd.
Knightsbridge
London SW1X 7XL
t. 020 7730 1234
www.harrods.com

Harvey Nichols
100–125 Knightsbridge
London SW1X 7RJ
t. 0870 8873 3833
www.harveynichols.com

Hèrmes
155 New Bond Street
London W1S 2UA
t. 020 7499 8856
www.hermes.com

JP Tod's
35–6 Sloane Street
London SW1X 9LP
t. 020 7235 1321

Liberty Plc.
Regent Street
London W1R 6AH
t. 020 7734 1234
www.liberty.co.uk

Linda Bee
Grays Antique Market
26 South Molton Lane
London W1K 5AB
t/f. 020 7629 5921

Louis Vuitton
t. 020 7399 4050 for stores
www.louisvuitton.com

Lulu Guinness
3 Ellis Street
London SW1X 9AL
t. 020 823 4828
www.luluguinness.co.uk

Miu Miu
123 New Bond Street
London W1S 1EJ
t. 020 7409 0900

Oasis
69–77 Paul Street
London EC2A 4PN
t. 020 7452 1000 for stores
www.oasisstores.com

Osprey
11 St Christopher's Place
London W1U 1NG
t. 020 7935 2824

Parallel
22 Marylebone High Street
London W1M 3PE
t. 020 7224 0441

Prada
16–18 Old Bond Street
London W1S 4PS
t. 020 7235 0008 / 7647 5000

Selfridges & Co.
400 Oxford Street
London W1A 1AB
t. 020 7629 1234
& 1 The Dome
The Trafford Centre
Manchester MI7 8DA
t. 0161 629 1234
www.selfridges.co.uk

Tanner Krolle
38 Old Bond Street
London W1S 4QP
t. 020 7491 2243
www.tannerkrolle.com

Top Shop
t. 0870 122 8808 for stores
www.topshop.co.uk

credits & acknowledgements

key: *a*=above, *b*=below, *l*=left, *r*=right, *c*=centre

Special photography: Chris Everard
Other photography by:
Chris Drake: *53*
Chris Everard: *8; 14; 16; 19; 20; 24; 27; 30; 32; 36; 37; 47; 50; 56; 59; 60*
Catherine Gratwicke: *2 & 7* VV Rouleaux, Ribbons, Trimmings and Braids; *4-5* Martin
Barrell and Amanda Sellers' flat, owners of Maisonette, London; *23 & 41; 42* Lulu
Guiness's house in London
Tom Leighton: *38*
Debi Treloar: *12* Ben John's and Deb Waterman, John's house in Georgetown
Pia Tryde: *44; 48*
Alan Williams: *54*
Andrew Wood: *28*
Polly Wreford: *10; 35*

Huge thanks to Fiona for sharing her divine collection of handbags (and hat!) with the
world. We're all jealous!

The author and publisher would also like to thank everyone who made the photography
for this book possible. Grateful thanks to Parallel and Linda Bee for loaning items for
photography.

Special thanks to Debbie, Emma, Darcey, and to Jo Blyth and little Emily for modelling.